WHEN MOMMY SAYS GOODNIGHT TO THE STARS

By: Erik Usher

This book is dedicated to all the families of those First responders who selflessly spend nights away from their families to help yours.

More importantly, this is for my wonderful wife who had to answer this questions to our two children Maya and Max!

"When Mommy Says Goodnight to The Stars"
Copyright © 2024 by Erik Usher

All rights reserved. No part of this publication may be reproduced or transmitted in any form or by any means, electronic or mechanical, Including photocopying, recording or any information storage and retrieval system, without written permission from the copyright owner.

"Why isn't Mommy home tonight?" asked Maya, hugging her favorite stuffed dog tightly. The soft glow of her bedside lamp lit up the room as she gazed at Daddy with curious eyes.

"Well, Maya," said Dad, tucking her in, "Mommy is out helping people tonight. She's a Police Officer, and that means she's always ready to protect people when they're in trouble."

"Is Mommy chasing bad guys?" Maya asked, her eyes wide.

"Sometimes," Dad said with a nod. "But mostly, Mommy is helping people—like finding someone who's lost or making sure everyone gets home safely."

"Does Mommy ever get scared?" Maya whispered.

"Sometimes," Dad said softly. "But Mommy is very brave. She has special training to stay calm and make the right choices, even when things are hard."

"Does Mommy think about me when she's at work?" Maya asked.

"Always," said Dad. "She says you're her little spark of courage. Thinking of you makes her brave, even on the toughest nights."

"But why does she have to work at night?"

"Because some people need help most when the world is quiet and asleep," Dad explained. "Mommy works so that other families can feel safe, just like you do here at home."

"Will she come home soon?" Maya asked as she yawned.

"Yes, sweetheart," Dad said, pulling the blanket snug around her. "And when she does, she'll be so happy to see you. She loves hearing about your dreams."

That night, Maya dreamed of her mom driving her police car under the stars, helping people stay safe. Even though she wasn't home, she knew she was a hero, and the stars were watching over both of them.

Pictures of my Mom

Pictures of me and my Mom

Drawings of my Mom

My favorite things about my Mom

Drawings of my Mom at work

Drawings of Mom and Dad

Drawings of Dad tucking me in

My favorite things about my Dad

www.ingramcontent.com/pod-product-compliance
Lightning Source LLC
Chambersburg PA
CBRC090840010526
44119CB00045B/502